By His Grace... Here I Am

BY

Carmen Greenard-Varnum

Editor: Angela M. Smith – Nataph Consulting
NataphConsulting@outlook.com

Cover designed by: Ellis & Ellis Consulting Group, LLC
www.ellisandellisconsulting.org

Author Photo: David Price Photography
pricelessphotosatl@gmail.com   443-909-6977

By His Grace... Here I Am
ISBN 9798457544437
(P) & © 2021
Carmen Varnum
carmenvarnum@yahoo.com

ABOUT THE AUTHOR

Carmen Y. Greenard-Varnum

Born into the foster care system and years later adopted by my foster parents, life wasn't easy for me. But I endured and overcame the hardships that come with being fostered. My desire to live a better life than what I learned led me to a 35-year successful career in the financial industry. My greatest achievement is being a wife and mother to the three most beautiful children that God gifted me. I was blessed to watch them grow to become loving, caring, and educated adults. Currently, I am the Mom Manager of my youngest son, Jonathan Greenard, who is cultivating his career in the NFL - #52 for Houston Texans. At the age of 54, *By His Grace, Here I Am* - living my best life.

CHAPTER 1

IN THE BEGINNING

On October 24, 1967, I was born in Atlanta, Georgia, and placed into foster care unto adoption by my foster parents. My biological mother was 14-years old when she had me and was not able to take care of me. My foster parents were an older couple who had four adult biological children. This couple decided to start fostering kids. When I was 5-years old, they decided to adopt me, so this became my permanent home. I have a vivid memory and remember as far back as when I started kindergarten. I remember crying all the time and my kindergarten teacher shushing me to be quiet. At that time, kindergarten was a half-day of school from 7:30 a.m. to 12:00 noon. Also, I remember that I always felt isolated; I was quiet and stayed to myself. Later, my parents began to get more foster kids, temporarily; they were coming and going.

There was a family of three siblings she fostered who were a significant part of my journey. They were Janice (she had some beautifully textured hair like most, if not all, biracial children), Chris, and Terrance. I shared a bedroom with the Janice and her brothers shared a room next to ours. They stayed with us for about four, maybe five years. Our home environment was strict and extremely disciplined. My adopted father (Horace) was a pastor, retired military, and owned a small neighborhood grocery store. He worked a lot, and he let her handle everything at home.

My adopted mother (Della) was a hairstylist by trade, a housewife, and a used to be alcoholic. From time to time, she would also run the grocery store with my adoptive father. My mother had nice clothes. She loved to dress nice, smell good, and makeup her face every day before leaving the house. She was definitely the disciplinarian in the home; was small, short statue-type woman and always had a mean look on her face. To tell you the truth, I was afraid of her, so I did whatever she said.

Throughout the years, my parents argued, fussed, and fought like any other couple. They argued almost every night about this, that, or the other. It was always something. My mother was a person who held boiling water under the lid really good. You just never knew when she was going to lash out. At any moment, literally any moment, she would explode because the issues were overpowering her. So, for me, I pretty much walked on eggshells around her. At some point, she began to be mentally and physically abusive towards me. A child in every way, I didn't understand why she behaved the way she did. However, the more I matured in life the better I understood the "why" behind her behaviors.

We had what appeared to be an unchanging ritual of get up and eat breakfast, then, get dressed and go to school. After school, we came home, did our homework, ate dinner; we might have a chance to go outside and play if it wasn't dark, or look at TV for about two hours, then get ready for bed. On Saturday mornings, we got up around 7:00 a.m., ate breakfast, then did our yard work like cutting the grass, trimming hedges, pulling up weeds, raking the yard, etc. Our house sat on a 4-acre corner lot – we had a huge yard. We would be in the yard as early as 8:00 a.m. until 1:00 p.m. Afterwards, we would come in and clean up and kind of chill for a while or go outside and play. We had a very structured life. We had chores almost every day of the week. But there were things that other students were involved in that I wanted to participate in, but I couldn't because my mother wouldn't allow me especially if there's a cost.

School activities, i.e., football games, basketball games, dances, or parties of any sort were out of the question. However, the one thing that I did participate in was music – I was in the school chorus. For some reason, I really enjoyed singing. It was an outlet for me to express my feelings. Other than that, it was school, church, or home. I didn't mind it being the way it was, but I still wanted to be social and participate in other extracurricular activities like my friends in the neighborhood did. But, since it was not permitted, I didn't sweat it. Like the old saying, you can't miss something you never had.

On Sundays, we did morning breakfast and then got ready for church. We had Sunday School at 9:00 a.m., Sunday morning service at 10:45 a.m., and Sunday evening service at 7:00 p.m. Then, we'd go to Wednesday night bible study at 6:30 p.m. After doing this for so long, it naturally became a part of my life. One Sunday evening my foster mother was testifying about how God had blessed her. She talked about her foster children and the one she adopted and called out our last names, Owens, Nelms, etc. After church, when we got in the car, I asked her who Nelms was because I knew the other foster kids' last names. She told me that Nelms was my previous last name before I was adopted, and then it changed to Daniel. That's how I found out I was adopted. I knew I was different, and this explained it. I was glad that they told me. Very curious, I started to ask more questions about my adoption, and she explained to me that my mother was a product of the foster care system herself and got pregnant with me when she was 14 years old, and I was born prematurely at seven months.

My foster mother agreed to care for me until my mother was able to get me back. So, I was placed in their home a few weeks after I was born. She said that due to my mother not receiving any prenatal care she was very sick after she delivered me, so she had to stay in the hospital for a while. Once my mother had gotten out of the hospital, they allowed her to visit me with a social worker. She came to visit me two times. When I was about three, my foster parents received a call that my mother was placing me up for adoption. My foster mother said that she was disappointed because she wanted my biological mother to take me back. Parents, in general, naturally show love and affection towards their children. However, I never received this love and affection from my foster mother. Even though she didn't birth me, she was still a mother, and I was still a child.

At school I was always picked on because I was dark-skinned, very solemn-looking, and had short hair - looked like a boy. Despite being picked on, school is where I felt like I could be a child simply because I was around children. Nonetheless, after a while, I began to come out of that solemn look stage and started to smile and interact with other children. I also remember going to the social worker's office frequently. Later in life, when I obtained a copy of my adoption records it showed that a caseworker was following up on me every month until the age of seven. They were making sure my motor and developmental skills were up to par.

I always felt different... like an outsider because I didn't feel the love as a child, i.e. receiving hugs, being told I was love, being told I was beautiful, etc. As far as I was concerned, I was only merely existing. I felt like an outcast; that I didn't fit in with that family. I did not look like them, I grew taller than them, and my feet were large.

It was very hard for my mom to find shoes that fit. Sometimes, I would wear my shoes a little bit longer, even if they were on the wear-and-tear side. Also, my mother shopped at the thrift store for my clothes. I always wore blue jeans, a t-shirt, and tennis shoes (to this day, I wear very few jeans and tennis shoes). I watched her get dressed in nice fashions, and I wanted to have the same, but she would never buy me the finer clothes. The only time that I would dress up would be when we were going to church. I just wanted to fit in a space of normalcy.

I can remember one day in the fifth grade, in Ms. Spencer's class (she was about eight months pregnant), the students were picking at me, and she did not advocate for me and stop them. She pretty much laughed with them. A student asked Ms. Spencer what she would do if her baby came out looking like me. She told them she was going to leave it at the hospital. They all burst out laughing! The pain was indescribable. I turned my head and acted like I didn't hear them or see them laughing. It is a downright shame that some of the teachers were just as cruel as the students. Like always, I just endured it.

After that, Ms. Spencer was out for a couple of weeks. Then, one day I overheard another teacher mention that she was on medical leave due to a miscarriage. The teacher told another teacher that she was reaching up in the cabinet to get something, and the umbilical cord got wrapped around the baby's neck. They probably thought I wasn't paying attention to their conversation, but I, sure enough, heard it all. I felt so bad for Ms. Spencer because she was so far along. A few months later, Ms. Spencer returned to the classroom, and she looked different. Her demeanor was different, and she never said much to me anymore.

On another note, I never had a birthday party as a child. On my 10th or 11th, I thought I had a cake because it was in a small square-shaped lavender box. When I opened the box, it was a little curly Afro wig. YES! You read correctly! A WIG! Mind you, my foster mother was a hairstylist, but she would never do anything to my hair. SHE BOUGHT ME A WIG! She would put a ribbon on the top to match whatever color outfit I had on. I was horrified because the children on the school bus teased me. They would snatch that wig off my head and throw it across the bus. I finally hid the thing and told my mom that somebody took it and I couldn't find it.

Anyway, going to church was also an escape for me. I enjoyed going to church like I did a good football game. Around the age of 11, my mother put me in the youth choir for the Easter Sunday service. I enjoyed being around others my age, singing, laughing, and just having a good time. To this day, I sing for the Lord. At the age of 14, I got saved and accepted Jesus Christ as my Lord and Savior. I remember, during Sunday school, I didn't talk because I was afraid the teacher would ask me questions when I didn't understand. I didn't want all eyes on me. However, after I started to study the Bible, I began to follow along and understand the lessons better. One Sunday morning, my pastor preached from the same subject that my Sunday school teacher taught. This tag-team, of the sort, captured my attention.

One Sunday evening, Janice and her brothers saw their aunt (their mother's sister) at church, and they were so excited. They got her phone number and communicated with her from time to time. During the time they were with us, the issues my mother had with my father intensified. Not only was he a pastor, but he was also a womanizer. My mother had put up with a lot of his foolishness and transgressions to the point she was very insecure around any other woman. She was especially mean to Janice.

One night, my dad came into our room and started to molest Janice (she was about 15 and I was 13). I heard her frantically moaning and telling him to stop; I told him to leave her alone! When I said something, he would slowly walk out of the room. It was like I was her protector because I would always tell him to leave her alone before I tell Mama, and he would run out as if he hadn't done anything.

So, one Saturday evening, my mother was cooking Sunday dinner - as they would do back in the day, I was in my bedroom, my two foster brothers were in the other room, and Janice was in the living room on the sofa watching television. Out of nowhere, I heard my mother hollering at my father as he was walking out the door. My father had thrown something at Janice, and my mom saw it. She looked at Janice and asked her what he threw at her. Janice said she didn't know. When she picked up the object, my mom snatched it out of her hand. It was a folded $20 bill.

My mother screamed at her, went, and got her gun, and started shooting at my dad as he left the house to get to his car. I was distraught! Then, she went into the kitchen and came out with a large butcher knife and cut off Janice's two long beautiful pigtails, threw them in the trash, and called her a heffa. Janice was screaming hysterically! I felt so horrible for her I could have died! Janice ran down the hall to our room and dived on the bed crying, uncontrollably. I was trembling and crying with her. Adding insult to injury, my mom came in and started beating on her, hitting me a few times. I was in shock - scared to death - because I didn't know what would happen to either one of us. The following morning, my mother cut the rest of Janice's hair off with the scissors – it was low to the head.

This incident led to the beginning of them running away one-by-one. Janice had contacted her aunt, and obviously, it had to do with how they were treating her. One day she went to school and didn't come home. Afterward, her brother, Chris, – never came home after school. Finally, the last brother, Terrance, did the same thing. For a while, my mother did not report it to the Department of Family and Children Services (DFCS), and she continued to receive checks for them. At some point, I know the aunt reported it to DFCS because they came to our home to investigate. I didn't understand how that process worked, but they never came back. And I? I was left alone to continue to experience hell and abuse from my mother.

Each day got worse after Terrance left. We were a year apart and attended the same school. One day, he asked if I would bring a pair of his pants and shoes that he left at the house. Of course, I thought nothing of it. So, when I got home, I put them in a brown paper bag so I wouldn't forget them. The next day, I was headed out the door for school with that brown paper bag in my hand. As I was walking down the walkway, my mother called me back in to ask what I had in that bag. When I got in the house, she was fussing and snatched that bag out of my hand. I told her it was a pair of pants and shoes that Terrance left and asked me to bring them to him.

Soon as I turned around to go back out of the house, she hit me in the back of my head with a broomstick. I fell out of the door crying and screaming. It felt like my head was busted wide open. She slammed the door, and I walked to the bus stop (at the end of our front yard) sobbing. The other kids waiting for the bus were looking on, and nobody said a word. Although they saw that one incident, I guarantee you that they had no idea the living hell my life was. I used to cry and pray, hoping my biological mother would one day come and get me.

For now, though, I had to learn how to adjust to my situation until I could do better. To me, love had nothing to do with my foster mom fostering children in need. It was all about the money. Throughout the years, I would always question God why? Why my biological parents didn't want me, why was I given up, why was I brought here, why did I have to stay here, why didn't they love me, why didn't they show love to me, why were teachers at school and other students always picking on me why? Why was I ugly?

WHY?!?!?! WHY?!?!?! WHY?!?!?!

There were times in my life I would shut down for weeks. I couldn't speak to anyone. I barely acknowledged them because I went into a dark place of feeling unwanted. I felt like the foster care system had royally failed me in so many ways - I lie not, I wanted to die. In school, it was hard for me to focus on my studies sometimes. I didn't feel smart like the other kids because my mother never sat down and studied with me or helped me with homework. When they say, 'every man for himself,' it was me for me. I was on my own, figuring this thing out. No child should have had to live like this, but I, and many other foster kids, did! There were times I wanted to report them to the caseworker who came to check on the other foster kids. I just wanted to be the tattle-teller and tell them EVERYTHING! But I knew if I said one word, we would have been taken away.

Only God knows where they would have placed us, either in another foster home or an orphanage. As a matter of fact, there were quite a few students who lived in an orphanage near our school, and I came to find out that the orphanage wasn't as bad as I thought it was. The ideal orphanage, to me, was something that I saw on television, and that was all bad. But this place was very nice! The kids there got new clothes, new shoes, and they loved their dorm mother. I learned this from speaking with some of the students that were in my class. They all had family issues with different dynamics. Whatever happened with their parents forced them into the orphanage, and they seemed to have it much better than I did.

I was at home with my family, but they didn't love me. My mother would get upset and call me all sorts of awful names, like a whore, and a liar. I never understood why she would call me those filthy names. I even asked her one day, and she answered with her fist: beating me upside the head for questioning her. It got so bad I would question God, and I started to wonder if He was even real. I know that He is, now, but as a child, I didn't know how to explain these evil things that people were doing to me.

On June 5, 1985, I graduated high school at the age of 16. Back in the day, you had to be five years old to start kindergarten. For some reason, I got in early and started at four years old. Anyways, my parents didn't come to my high school graduation. We had three cars, and I begged her to come. I was almost late because I had to ride the bus; I hated her for that! I asked her why she adopted me, and she told me she didn't know. I just walked away in sadness. I was determined to get out of this toxic environment and live better. College was the way to do that, and I was going to get there somehow in some way.

Since I was young, I loved singing and knew that I could sing. So, I was awarded a partial scholarship in music (I auditioned and joined the Gospel choir) at a college in Tuscaloosa, Alabama. I wanted to become a music teacher.   Before arriving at college that fall, I worked the entire summer at Krystal's, my very first job, trying to save up some money to get me through the first school year. I went down on a Greyhound bus with one suitcase and a black garbage bag with some clothes in it. My foster mom was adamant about me not going anywhere and not being anything. But I sarcastically assured her, oh yes; yes, ma'am, I am!

When I initially got on campus, I was nervous and excited. And guess who I saw? My foster brother, Terrance. It was like a dream come true; someone was there who knew me, and I was not alone! We hugged and chatted for a while and acted as if we were brother and sister. In a way, we were. So, that's what we told everyone. He looked out for me on campus, you know, financially, helping me when my little funds ran out. It was refreshing to have someone there for me. We stayed in contact for a very long time until his passing away many years later.

There was an incident on campus where my music professor tried to rape me. I was scared for my life as I fought him off and got away. When I called my mom to explain what was happening, her response made me feel that she did not care. I tell you the truth; I don't know what I was thinking by going to her about this situation. She was talking to me as if it was my fault that he attacked me. As if I encouraged him: *Hey! Come over here and rape me! I'm gon' turn you on so you can brutally take advantage of me.* Like, who wants to be a rape victim? Anyways, on top of that, I did not finish college. My financial dilemma put me in real hardship.

When I went to take my final exams, I learned that I had a tuition balance due. Well, I could not take final exams with a tuition balance. Then, YES... then, I was told that there was no partial scholarship. NO SCHOLARSHIP to take care of my tuition. Even after financial aid and student loans had been applied to my account, my dollars were not plenty to pay the out-of-pocket cost. So, I ended up leaving school and going back to Atlanta. Some friends loaned me the money, and I bought a bus ticket home. I called my foster mom and told her that I was coming home; I could not afford to stay in school. She let me come back, though, but it was under the conditions that I get a job and pay $350.00 a month for rent.

~ MY FIRST MARRIAGE ~

There was no way I was going to be able to do that right away. However, I did find a job at Kmart across town, and within two months, I found an apartment and moved out. I had to do what I was going to do quickly because staying with her long-term was not an option. While working at Kmart, I met a young man named Jacob, who was a frequent shopper. We began to have conversations that ultimately turned into something a bit serious. We were young folks (I was 19, and he was 21). Green as summer grass about life, I got pregnant - so we got married. Marrying so early turned out to be a big mistake in my life. Shoot! You now! I just wanted somebody to show me genuine love, something I had never experienced. We were young virgins – well, I know I was and thought he was – having fun.

On New Year's Eve, 1986, we partied into the new year. While celebrating, I got sick and almost fainted. That following Monday morning, we went to see what was going on with me - I was nine weeks pregnant. OMG! I was shocked about the pregnancy, but I was keeping this baby, honey! I was headstrong about breaking a cycle of giving up children. My child would never experience foster care and abuse like I did. On March 14, 1987, we went to the courthouse and got married. We were happy and excited about this adult move of love and family. But, shortly afterward, the marriage started to go downhill. My husband was having an affair.

How did I find out he was cheating? After my five months OB appointment, the hospital was consistently calling me at work. At the time, I had given them my home address, and phone number where I grew up, and my work number. When they couldn't reach me at home, they would call my job, but I kept missing their call. One day my supervisor pulled me to the side and told me that the calls were from the health department. Young and naive, I still had no clue. My manager took me to her office, closed the door, and told me that I needed to call them right then. I returned the call, and they asked me to come in immediately, so I did.

When I got there, they said my test results from my prenatal visit came back positive for Gonorrhea and Chlamydia. Then, they asked if I had any other sexual partners, and, of course, the answer was an absolute NO! Look-a-here, I was shattered and afraid. The doctor told me that I needed to take Penicillin, and it could cause harm to the baby if I continued with the pregnancy. I had no one to call and talk to about this, so I just took the pills. And to think – that negro did not have the decency to tell me that he had an STD AND that he had gotten himself checked and cleared with medication.

Later on that night, I started having contractions that were a steady 30-minutes apart. And, as usual, my husband was in the streets as I endured these pains all night long. I prayed and cried myself to sleep; by the morning, the contractions had stopped. When I got up, I called the nurse and explained what had happened during the night. She stated that if it happened again to go to the hospital. Well, I am thankful that it never happened again, and I was able to carry the pregnancy full-term. However, shortly after I confronted my husband about the STDs, we got into a big fight.

From that point, the marriage kept getting worse. I continued to stay in the apartment, and he kept on cheating. During this fiasco, I caught him in the bed with another woman, almost had a nervous breakdown, lost a lot of weight, and my hair fell out. I cried every day, but I still wore my crown, got up and caught the bus, took my baby to the babysitter, went to work, came back home, and did it again! I couldn't give up on life because my daughter was the most important thing to me! I loved her, and I was going to take good care of her. She was mine, and I was hers.

The final straw was when one Friday night when Jacob had been out in my car. The next day, we were headed to a basketball game and stopped to get gas. When he went inside to pay, I picked up something off the passenger side floormat that looked like a card of some sort. It was another female driver's license, and I recognized her photo. When he got back in the car, I addressed the situation, and we immediately got into an argument. When we came to a red light, he punched me in my face. While we were fighting, my daughter (9-months old at this time) was screaming to the top of her lungs. He finally stopped the car in the middle of the road and got out, yelling at me. He said that he was going to kill me.

As he was coming around to the passenger side, I locked the doors, climbed into the driver's seat, and took off. I knew I needed to get away quickly. I was hurting, and my mind was racing, trying to figure out who I could turn to for help. There was no one! Since he continued to abuse and disrespect me by laying with other women and laying hands on me, I started seeking a way to get out of this disaster. This 1 ½ year of marriage was a hard lesson learned. Eventually, I got help from a Legal Aid Attorney who did my divorce pro bono and assisted me with getting child support for a while.

After that, I left Jacob and NEVER looked back. At the end of it all, I found another apartment on my own, but I had to wait three weeks before moving in because it wasn't ready yet. They were running a special, so I got it for a low monthly rent with no deposit. For those next three weeks, though, I needed somewhere to stay. I was desperate, so I called home and asked my mom if I could PLEASE come home for that time. Begging and pleading my case, she said yes.

I moved all my personal belongings – except for what I needed during those three weeks – into storage. I was exhausted after moving my things and arrived at my parent's place about 9:30 p.m. that night. It took a while to get there because I lived on the Northside of Atlanta, and they lived on the Southwest side. When I got there, my dad opened the door, greeted me, and grabbed the baby out of my arms. I went down the hall to their bedroom and told my mother that I was there.

She was on her side, and she never turned around to acknowledge me. As I turned to go to my old bedroom, she called my name and told me that she had changed her mind and that I could not stay in her house. She raised her voice a notch – I guess to make sure that I clearly understood that I was not welcomed there – and reiterated that I COULD NOT stay in her house. I looked at her in disbelief, immediately got my daughter, and got out of there as fast as I could.

My father was trying to talk to her, to let her know that she was wrong for changing her mind. She got angry and stormed towards me as I was running out the door. She came to the door hollering and cursing – I just put my baby back in her car seat and left. Whatever it was going on with her, I wasn't going to stay to find out. It was just too much! Thankfully, I still had the key to my old apartment. I wasn't going to turn the key in until the next day, but I ended up going back to that empty apartment and sleeping on the floor for two nights. I was afraid and just utterly taken back by the way my mother treated me. I contacted the apartment manager at the new place and begged her to let me move in sooner. I told her my situation, and she finally agreed.

At that very moment, I cared nothing about them having to repair that apartment while I was in it – I was concerned about our safety and making it the next 24 hours. You know, "survival mode." I thank God that I had a childcare giver who was understanding and worked with me because there were times, I barely had enough money for food, let alone daycare. The owner was very kind to me. When I had it, I paid for it! But I made sure I didn't get too far behind. These were some hard times for me, but I was surviving.

One day when I was headed to work, I ran into an old friend that I knew from high school. His name was Washington, and this is how we initially met.

THINKING OUT LOUD: Some years ago, when I was way younger, I had previously met him over to my adopted parents' son's house. He was a high school friend of their son. It was a Christmas season and family would go over to each other's house. My adoptive mom wanted to go to her son's house in Decatur and we went. When I got there, I asked where my nephew was and was told he was downstairs with some of his football friends. I went downstairs to say hello and when I got down there, I saw a whole bunch of big boys. I was very nervous because I had never had a boyfriend, and I was afraid of boys at that time.

My mom would never let me have a boyfriend in high school. So I said hello and I ran back upstairs. A couple days later after seeing his friend he wanted my phone number and my nephew called me during the week and gave it to me. When I was in high school and my mother would be at work, I would sneak and call him from time to time, so we had a chance to talk to each other for a while. When I graduated high school, and right before I left to go to college, I caught the bus one Saturday and went over to see him. He told me he was so infatuated with me because I had my mind made up of what I wanted out of life. He said that he was so intrigued by me to he had never met anyone that knew what they really wanted out of life. He didn't try anything, we just talked and looked through the yearbook that I took with me.

When I was in college, I did call him a couple of times a couple of times but eventually that communication faded away. So, when I came back from college, I had *moved on the other side of town and that's when I had met my daughter's father, Jacob.*

When he saw me, he was so excited! He didn't work far from where I lived, and he asked if he could he visit. Of course, I said yes. I didn't have a phone at the time, so I did give him my address and one Thursday afternoon he stopped by after work. My daughter was in the room asleep, and we sat there for a minute watching TV and talking about old times from high school; just catching up on what we had going on in our lives. While he was sitting there someone knocked on the door. I couldn't imagine who it could've been because I had just moved there, and I didn't know anyone. Well... it was Jacob. He was knocking really hard, and I said who is it and he demanded me to open the door. I asked him what he wanted because we're not married anymore.

Again, he, very demanding, told me to open the door. I didn't open the door, so he bust the door in and started choking me. I fell against the wall and by this time Washington was coming to my rescue and they got into a violent fight. I was screaming; I didn't know what to do because I didn't have a phone.

However, somebody in the complex heard what was going on and they called the police. Jacob was arrested, Washington's hand was bleeding (it was cut on the broken glass from the dinette table), and I was completely embarrassed – just stupid and unnecessary drama. It was almost as if Jacob was stalking me and knew that I had a man in the house. I didn't know what to say to Washington, but I wanted to make sure he was okay. The paramedics checked him out, and he was.

I was shook – just baffled – and told him I think it's best that he doesn't come around for now. I needed to get my life together and I did not want him to get hurt or killed in the process. So I didn't see Washington anymore until I divorced my second husband and moved into my second home.

CHAPTER 2

THROUGH THE STORM

One Wednesday in March of 1992, I was getting dressed for work, and I got a call from my foster mom. I was shocked being that we hadn't spoken in about two years. However, I used to talk to my dad from time to time to let him know that I was okay. That's how she got my phone number because I never spoke to her once after I left that house. She never made attempts to see me, buy pampers, milk or anything to help out. So I was surprised to hear her voice when I answered my phone. She asked the general how you are doing, how the baby doing and when are you going to bring the baby over kinds of questions. I was never one to disrespect or talk back to her out of fear; so, I just said I'll bring her by that weekend. She said okay and then I told her I was getting ready for work, and I got off the phone.

As I was getting in the car, I hit my knee on the car door and I tore my stockings. I went back into the house to change because it was a dress code requirement to wear pantyhose with your dresses or skirts at work. When I went back in the house, I saw my answering machine flashing wondering who else could have called that quick. I checked the message, and it was my foster dad telling me to call home immediately. Upon calling, he said your mom just passed; she had a massive heart attack. At that moment I was shocked because I literally had just gotten off the phone with her.

My father explained that when she got off the phone with me, she turned sideways and made a sound as if she was choking and coughing at the same time. He said that he called out her name and she didn't respond. The second time he called her name he leaned over to check on her and she didn't move. He immediately started CPR trying to revive her; when it didn't work, he called 911. I told him that I'd be over there shortly. So, I took my daughter to the daycare and went there. When I got there my foster mom's daughter and son were there.

My father was in the room with other relatives who had come over. The daughter and son were there and never spoke to or even acknowledged me. I knew something wasn't right. They were already in the bedroom writing an obituary to take to the funeral home. They never consulted me on anything. I stayed back and didn't say anything and eventually I left. I didn't know how to feel or react because of what I had been going through with her, but I still went and paid my respects.

Another relative was the one who told me the date of the funeral because the daughter never gave me any information. On the day of the funeral all immediate family members we're gathered at the house to follow the hearse to the church. As the cars were lining up, there were two family cars, from the funeral home, for immediate family members to ride in. The gentleman from the funeral home called out the names of the individuals who should get in the family limousines. He called my dad's name first, the daughter, the biological son, the grandchildren, and some other family members. He never called my name.

I stood there in disbelief, and I wanted to cry because I already knew what had happened. My father saw me standing there and he got out the car and asked me why I didn't get in the family car. I told him they never called my name. My father called his daughter and she got out the car and he asked her why she didn't put my name on the list to get in the family car. She replied, I thought she was driving her own car. I was pissed and my father told me to get into the front seat with him.

On the ride to the church I just didn't know how to feel because I was left out of everything. As we walked inside, I sat quietly in the back and started reading over the program and looking at the pictures inside. At the end of the obituary, after acknowledging the family friends, they had my name at the very end as one adopted child, Carmen. I was beyond hurt!!! This was the only family that I ever knew and to be ostracized like that was traumatic. After the funeral, everyone was gathered outside talking and then prepared to go to the cemetery.

When we got to the cemetery there were four chairs in front of the casket and there were some other chairs on the other side of the casket. I sat in one of the four chairs first. Come to find out those chairs was for my father and other relatives. Somehow the daughter was left standing. As she was standing, she came beside me on the end where I was sitting and started nudging me on the shoulder to get up. I refused and she kept nudging until I looked up at her and I said, *"If you touch me one more time, I'm going to throw you in the damn hole with your mama."* I said it kind of loud because someone heard us and came over to pull us apart. So guess what? She had to stand up.😂😂😂😂 (laughing).

After the final prayer and they lowered my mother's body to the ground, we greeted folks and then went back to the house for a repass. I tried to, and I genuinely wanted to, keep in touch with my father after this. However, the daughter wouldn't allow me to visit. She stated that my mom did so much for the foster kids, and she resented me. I was surprised that she said this to me because I was around her a lot growing up; I pretty much looked up to her. This statement is proof that you never know what someone is feeling about you, about something that is 100% out of your control. Also, since my parents were so much older, she was the one I would have lived with if something happened to them. For her to feel this way was shocking!

At this point, I coughed it up to reality and realized that it was just my daughter and me against the world, and I had to go on and do the best that I could to live a productive life.

~ MY SECOND MARRIAGE ~

In my young adult hood, I made sure I made safe choices for me and my daughter because no matter what I did if it was the wrong choice, it would affect her, and I didn't want anything to happen to her. She was so important to me! When my daughter was still a toddler, I started dating a gentleman, Sam, from my childhood neighborhood – very cute man if I say so myself. He was five years older than I, and I've always had a slight crush on him growing up. However, I couldn't tell anyone because I wasn't allowed to date. We reconnected when my mother passed away. He had stopped by to give his condolences and we started talking.

He inquired about what I was doing in my life, and I told him that I was divorced with a daughter. He wanted to know what I did in my spare time, and, well, you know with a toddler there really isn't much spare time available. I told him I go to work and come home to my daughter. He asked if we could go out for drinks and dinner, and I said okay. So, we exchanged numbers and three weeks later he called, and asked if he could visit. I felt comfortable with him because we grew up in the same neighborhood, his mother was a good childhood neighbor, and a teacher at the elementary school I attended.

Before he got to my place, I had called a friend and told her that this guy was coming over and I gave her his name and a description of his vehicle. I told her if she didn't hear back from me before midnight to call 911. 😂😂 (laughing). Also, I had put my daughter to sleep because I didn't want her to see him there. I was very mindful of bringing strangers and other men around my daughter. When he got there, we talked in the living room for a while about old times and people from the neighborhood. He left at a respectable time and asked if we could go out one evening with my daughter.

I thought that was very nice of him to acknowledge my child. It was a package deal simple as that. When we finally went out, I was nervous because I didn't know how my daughter would respond. She took to him really good and that was the icing on the cake for me. We continued to date and a year later he asked me to marry him; I was 23 years old, and he was 28. I was so excited and happy to be a wife again and believed that this time marriage was going to be successful because he was a mature man. We eventually had my second child – a son, and four years later we had another son.

Things were going good for us until a big shift shifted the atmosphere. By the time I had my third child my marriage was failing because of Sam's drinking and hanging out, and he was not really contributing to the household. My husband had old ways like an older man, and I didn't mind because I was used to being a homebody making sure the house clean, dinner cooked, clothes washed etc. He pretty much had it made with me because he kind of shaped me the way he wanted me to be for him. For example, in my neighborhood, a lot of the wives didn't work; whatever the husband said they did. So, if my husband didn't like my outfit, I'd change it. It was things like that... he had a lot of control over me until I had had enough.

Over the years I had dealt with a lot. There were times I wasn't happy, but unhappiness can be expected in any marriage. One day I noticed that he didn't look the same, it was something different about his body. He was losing muscle mass and I didn't question it at first, I just dismissed it. Every Thursday was payday, and he would give me money for the bills. This particular payday he stated that he could no longer give me the

39 | P a g e

amount that he was giving me before. He said he could only give me $120 a week.

WHAT?!?!

I tried to talk to him about it, but he refused to communicate, and things just got worse. I looked at him and asked him where he was going to live because we have three children, a mortgage, car note, insurance, groceries, the boys played recreational sports, extracurricular activities, and a little bit more so how was $120 going to take care of his part of the bills. He didn't answer, he walked off.

I knew then something wasn't right! I told him if he did that he could not live here. No explanations and to just walk off and not give good reasons was not acceptable. The next payday came and this time he didn't put the money in my hand like he normally would, he laid $120 on my nightstand the next morning before he went to work. I was asleep and saw it when I woke up. When I got up for work and saw that's all he left I called him, but he wouldn't answer the phone. I waited until he got home, and I told him that he had to leave. I don't know if this was a newfound standard that I had set for myself not to tolerate unsatisfactory actions from my husband or if this was a trauma triggered response from how I saw my foster parents' marriage and my first marriage. Whatever it was, it wasn't happening on my watch. So, we begin to argue, and I picked up the phone and called the sheriff's department. I asked them if I had someone in my house and I wanted them to leave what was I supposed to do.

The operator asked had there been any physical altercation and I told her, *"NOT YET!"* She told me if I felt like my life was in danger and any physical altercation occurred to call 911. I hung up the phone and about 15-minutes later two sheriff cars pulled up in my driveway. They came to my door and asked if I called, and I said yes. I told them I wanted him to leave, with no questions they told him to come outside and eventually he had to leave. Of course he was upset, but I didn't care because I have three children, a new home, car note, insurance, and bills. He decided to stop contributing to the household. Here I was again trying to figure things out on my own!

That Saturday morning, I laid in the bed, sobbing, trying to understand what just took place. By Monday, I still had not heard a peep out of him. So, I decided to put him out since he chose the streets. I put all of his clothes, and I do mean everything, in garbage bags, took them over to his mother's house - that's where he was staying - and put them on the back of one of his two trucks. I called him to let him know what I had done and that there was no need for him to come back to the house. I eventually ended up filing for a divorce.

He had proved to me that he had no intentions of owning up to the status of a husband; and, he had no intention to provide financially. We had already separated one time before, for a good four weeks, and he begged, pleaded, and apologized then, telling me that he would do better. Well, here we were, and things had only gotten worse!

During this time, I continued to live at the house and pay the bills. Everything was getting behind, past due, late, all of that! He wouldn't give me any child support until I went to court. Panicking, I eventually called a realtor to place the house on the market. The whole ordeal was overwhelming, but I was trying to be proactive because I did not want to lose the house and mess up my credit. Luckily the house was on the market for only three weeks before I got an offer. At closing, we (the buyer, attorneys, and myself) were sitting at the table, passing the papers around, and I burst into tears. Can you say, MELTDOWN? MELTDOWN! I had worked so hard to purchase this home that I had built from the ground up at 31 years old. This accomplishment meant so much to me! Selling it to prevent losing it was a dreadful experience.

One day I sat down in the living room with the kids and explained what was happening. I told them we had to move. Not only were we moving, but I was moving them from their comfort zone and away from their friends. It was very hard as I tried my best to stay in the same school district. I had a huge yard sale, and I pretty much sold everything because I could not take them to an apartment. I couldn't afford rent and storage, so I was even giving items away.

Once I sold everything, we packed up what was left, found an apartment, and moved in. During this time, my daughter was also entering her first year of college. Whatever money I had left, I paid for some college fees and books. I was determined to make it happen for her, and I did. You know, I didn't have this kind of support, and I know, first-hand, the struggle that came with wanting to pursue an education with zero support. She would not ever ride that struggle bus; it was not going to be part of her life's story.

After we got settled into this apartment, we had to, eventually, move again because someone had broken in and stole some things when I was at work. This whole ordeal didn't make sense to me because we lived in a gated community. But I was afraid when the officer said that someone had a key and that it was not a forced break-in! Really? I complained to the leasing office, and they allowed me out of my lease.

Thirteen years of marriage ended like this; I was exceedingly upset with Sam for a long time. I had loved him and was hoping and trying to work things out, but we – for whatever reason – couldn't get it together. Nonetheless, over time I found a program that helped homebuyers purchase homes with down payment assistance. I applied and got it! We moved within six months into a new home. It was farther out than I desired, but I was desperate to get my children back in a house and not an apartment. My first year in our new home was uneasy, but it was affordable and close to work, so I wasn't complaining.

~ MEETING MY BIRTH PARENTS ~

Not only did my adopted mother pass in 1992, I met Sam in 1992, but I also decided to look for my biological parents in 1992. A lot was going on as I was approaching my 25th birthday. But this was something I was so anxious about and had dreamed about for years. I had learned that DFCS had disclosed that the adoption records in Fulton County were open, and they were now assisting adoptees in locating their biological parents. I had to write a detailed letter stating that I wanted to meet my biological parents.

Once they received the letter, along with an application and picture, they would contact the biological parent. If the parents agreed to meet the child, DFCS would arrange for the reunion. This process took almost a year, but it happened to me. I saw it on TV and read about these things happening, but I never imagined it would happen for me. Once DFCS saw that I was committed to the process, they called my mom, and she agreed to meet with me.

When I got the letter from DFCS stating that they had contacted my mother, I had a heart full of emotions. I had gone through so much, yet it felt like a dream come true. The social worker called me and stated that my mother would be giving me a call. About a week later, I received that call while I was at work. I told some of my co-workers what was happening and that I was very nervous and excited. When I heard her voice, she sounded a lot like me. She was excited as we shared about ourselves. Then, we decided to meet face-to-face. I described what I looked like and what I'd have on so she wouldn't have any problems identifying me. We met up at a mall, and when she got out of the car, she had a strange look on her face.

As we talked, she told me the same things my foster mom said about her having me at 14 years old. However, she dropped a bomb on me. A neighborhood babysitter had raped her, and she thought that I was the rapist child. She wanted nothing to do with me because I would be a constant reminder of her abuser. Let alone there was no way they were going to let her keep me anyways. She said that she'd made a mistake, and from looking at me, she knew who my biological father was because I looked just like him. She didn't tell me who he was, but at that moment – it didn't even matter because my focus was on my relationship with her. The next day, she invited me to her home, and I met my sister. WOW!

I have a sister! There were a lot of other family members there as well. So there was some explaining to be told about this beautiful, tall, chocolate daughter standing in their presence.

Establishing a healthy relationship with her was very difficult. She had deep-rooted wounds that she had not dealt with, a lot of baggage from the past, and needed deliverance from generational curses. These issues were significant blockages! Trusting people was at an all-time low, so I was already reluctant to being vulnerable. I had two children when I met her, and my marriage to Sam wasn't up to par. He was happy and jealous at the same time about me meeting my mom. While I was making every effort to get to know her, I was also away from home a great deal. So this meant that the dynamics of my home life were changing. Sam and I argued about this from time to time, and I felt torn between my husband and mom. She wanted some of my time, and my husband just wanted me to be home even though he knew where I was.

While we were getting to know one another, the psychological impact was overwhelming because I felt like she did not accept me. Set in my way of doing things, she was trying to handle me, if you will, and I was not even having that - we were constantly bumping heads. I mean, we were both grown, so why not treat each other like an adult mother to an adult daughter. She would say things (intentional or not) that were hurtful to the core. And, she boasted about her life, how she finished college, and how she had this, that, and the other - braggadocious to me.

All that bragging made me feel a bit insecure. I felt like I was not good enough to be who I was - her daughter, her first-born daughter at that! There were times I resented being around her. There were so many thick layers to peel away. I was not emotionally prepared to deal with this and what was becoming of our reunion. One time, she told me that she didn't babysit, so in other words, don't ask her to watch my kids. That, in my opinion, was so inappropriate, especially in our situation.

Later on, when I was going through my divorce from Sam, I needed her more than ever. As long as she was positively present, I didn't care how she was there for me, but she wasn't. She was not able to be who I needed her to be – for me. But she was always there for other family members and my sister. She knew them; she was able to grow a life with them; she, perhaps, even loved them. Maybe I should have understood that, then.

Perhaps, I was more like a friend than a daughter and should not have pushed the daughter-mother thing. I'm not sure what I should have done, but what I do know is that this was hard work, and it was draining the life out of me.

I was stubborn, and I would not give in to things that she wanted me to do. Honestly, I did not like her and how she was treating me. On one occasion, we had not spoken for about six months, and then she called. The meeting did not go well because she couldn't accept that she was wrong – at least in my opinion, she was wrong. For what? She treated me differently from my sister, but that was somewhat understandable because she raised her all her life. But it would have been nice to receive a little bit of compassion and a lot of understanding. She also promised me some things and never came through on those promises. The little girl in me, the little girl she deserted, wanted something from her – consistency!

Many times, we would go out to dinner, and she would never pay for the meals. There was always an excuse of some sort like I forgot my purse. I believe she did this intentionally because it happened several times. I finally put a stop to those shenanigans. She wouldn't apologize for her manipulations and try to start fresh based on forgiveness. Without her taking responsibility and accepting this truth, our relationship would never work – and it didn't. Ultimately, she caused so much havoc in my life; it badly affected me and caused problems in my marriage until my husband did not like her either.

After my divorce, getting my life in order and taking care of my children was my focus. Things seemed to be going pretty well as I was settling in my second new home with my sons while my daughter was at college. After 20 years of working on this..., this thing called a mother and daughter relationship, I severed the ties that were starting to bind me, and I was, and still am, at peace about it. I've come to accept the truth that to everything, there is a season: a season to pursue something (meeting and attempting to establish a relationship with my birth mother), and a season to let that same something loose – because it wasn't a healthy improvement for my life.

When I was 25 years old my mother took me to see my biological father, where he worked, and that was my very first time meeting him. We spoke briefly and he gave me a hug. Nothing further transpired of this. Later on, I ran into him again when I had to go downtown to a building near the court house to get a copy of my marriage license. I did not know where he worked, at that time, but when I went inside the building, and through the security gate, I saw him standing outside of an office. When I realized it was him, I waved and went to speak to him. We greeted one another and he wanted to know what I was doing there. I told him that I had to obtain a copy of my marriage licenses. As we were talking, he was on-the-sly escorting me back to the elevator.

Once the elevator doors opened, he escorted me in and told me to have a good day. Like... REALLY! He had just escorted me OUT OF HIS PRESENCE as if he didn't want anyone to see us together... talking... merely saying, hello! I felt like crawling under the ground. I got on the elevator and went on about my business with tears in my eyes and thoughts that were making my heart hard concerning him. The pain from rejection is an awful feeling! I never forgot that feeling of, *"oh, you're just another customer;"* or *"let me help this stranger find her way."* He made no effort to get to know me and that was painful.

~ MY THIRD MARRIAGE ~

One day, while I was riding the transit to work, I saw someone who resembled an old friend named Washington. For a minute, I honestly thought it was him, and I was about to call his name until the gentleman turned around - it wasn't him. Washington was on my mind all day long, so I decided to look him up and found an address showing where he lived. It was his grandparent's address from our high school days. Not playing around with my intentions, I was bold and sent him a letter. Although it had been many years since we had seen one another or spoken, and the risk of a wife or girlfriend intercepting the letter was possible, I took that risk and am glad I did.

I had told him that if he was married, do not bother me; if he was not married, I wanted to hear from him. I mailed that letter on a Thursday, and that Sunday, as we were arriving at church service, I put my phone on vibrate, and immediately I felt an incoming call buzzing in. Although I did not recognize the phone number, I answered it anyway. It was his sister Connie! While she was talking, I tried to ask her how Washington was and if he was married. As soon as I said it, he came out of nowhere and said, "HI, CARMEN!" We laughed, and I quickly asked if I could get his number and call him when service was over. We both were excited! Look-a-here, during that service, I did not hear a word the preacher was saying; I was daydreaming about meeting Washington. So, after church, I stopped and got us some dinner and called him back. We talked for a while, and then he asked me if he could see me that same day. He said he had wanted to make sure that I was not crazy and beat down from, basically, the "*all my life I had to fight experiences*" that we had talked about on the phone. Nervous and all, I said yes!

Although my sons were old enough to stay home alone for a short time, I still called my daughter and a dear friend and told them that I was about to visit an old friend across town for a couple of hours. I gave them his address, phone number, and a physical description of him. I told them that if they didn't hear from me by a specific time to call 911. When I pulled up to his house and saw him come out the door, I was happy; very happy! After all these years, he looked pretty much the same. He was a little heavier than I expected; nevertheless, I was still glad to see him. When he saw me, he was so excited and told me that I was still beautiful. From that day, we started dating.

A significant change happened in our relationship on a day I had gone in for a scheduled mammogram at work (I worked at a hospital), and the results had some abnormalities. Because of this, I ended up having a needle biopsy done, and those results can take up to 15 days. Well, this whole ordeal was very unsettling. All I could think about were my children and what would happen if this abnormality was malignant. However, the day I went back for the results, Washington went with me. We were nervous, and I was crying a river over the unfavorable possibilities! But thanks be to God, the results were negative.

After we left the doctor's office, Washington took me to Walmart to pick up a few things. When we got in the car, he proposed to me. While I was doing my shopping, he was doing his – an engagement ring. Of course, I said YES! With no delay, we went straight to the courthouse where he worked (he was on the police force), got our marriage license, and got married right then. Yep!

Right after that negative biopsy, we sealed our relationship. He had it all set up. Everything was so smooth, and everybody was already in place. He told me that he always loved me, and now that the opportunity to be with me was here, he was never going to let me go. Those were the most beautiful words anyone has ever said to me. We have known each other since I was 16 years old. It's funny how we've come full circle and are now husband and wife. I was born into foster care and adopted at age five by the same family that fostered me.

At age 16, I graduated from high school, went to college for one year, and came home and started working. I've gone through three marriages, married at 19 and divorced at 21; married at 23 and divorced at 35; and married at 37 with three children. I'd finally found some stability and a person who loved us for who we were. He's someone I can grow with and love even more with time. This is how I felt being with Washington — HAPPY! I was happy; he was sho'nuf happy, and my children were happy for me.

Washington worked on the other side of town, so I sold my home and moved into his world — the suburbs in the inner city. It was a very different atmosphere, and I was primarily concerned about my children because their education was most important. I wanted to make sure they were in a productive, non-violent, encouraging learning environment. Things weren't working out in the school district there, and we were a little at odds about where to live when looking for another home. Again, I was firm in my thinking and living and was not settling for *less than better, where their* education was concerned. So he asked me what would make me happy. I told him that moving back to their old school district; their comfort zone would make me happy. He agreed, and we moved back across town while he commuted to work. It was a huge sacrifice for him, but it worked out in our favor in the later years.

Our marriage was tested and tried in the early stages. Six months into the marriage, some things took place at work that forcibly caused Washington to resign. He was devastated, and I was, to the best of my ability, was the shoulder for him to lean on until we could get through it. Just when we thought things were getting better, they kept getting worse. We decided to look for our dream home, and once we found it, the bank decided, the week of closing, that they did not want to give us the loan due to what was happening with my husband - it was primetime news in our city. The whole situation was a personal vendetta his employer had against him, and they were doing everything they possibly could to destroy his name, reputation, and character. We made the best of the situation – money was tight, but we got through it.

A year later, when he accepted a promotion to Interim Chief, lo-and-behold, here we were again in an employment situation. The same individual had it out for my husband and went to the media and complained. During this time, we were still looking for another home. However, because of this newsworthy event (it wasn't about not having money or steady employment), the bank decided not to give us the loan again! I wanted to fight it, but it would have taken so much time and money, something that we did not have to waste. We ended up moving into an apartment and not worry about another home for a while. Living and enjoying our lives and our children was the main focus. They were more important to us than what was going on.

Both of our sons played sports, and as they got older, Washington noticed that my youngest son had a natural talent for football. So, he took some film footage to a friend of his who was a scout. Within 15-minutes of him dropping off the film, the scout called him back with some solid advice on which way to go. We followed that advice when my son was in the 9th grade. Once he got into the 11th grade, he took off. Even though he was excelling on the football field, we had to take a step back. Why? Because I lost my focus. And losing focus is easy to do when your life is topsy-turvy. I wasn't doing my part in making sure that they were doing their part - keeping those grades up. So, I hired a tutor, drove across town every Saturday, and sat in my car during his tutoring session. I did what I needed to do and saw positive results. His failing grades improved, and so did his SAT and ACT scores.

THINKING OUT LOUD: Now, as young children, their father was still very involved in their lives. He even got along well with Washington. He took them to practice sometimes, and many times we were at the games together. Suddenly, my ex-husband got sick. We noticed how frail he was but didn't know what was wrong because he was very private about his health. One Friday evening in 2014, I got a call from my ex-sister-in-law saying that he had passed out and was in the hospital. The next day, I met with my ex-sister-in-law to see him, and he wasn't doing good at all. By that Sunday, he was in ICU; on that Monday, he passed away from congestive heart failure at 51. Speechless!

It happened so quickly and unexpectedly, and we were not psychologically prepared for his death. My daughter was married and 8-months pregnant; my oldest son was in college, and my baby boy was a senior in high school, and I think it took a toll on him the most. I had known Sam all my life. I still grieved, even though we were divorced. I was married to him for 13 years! He was the father of my children! I loved him dearly and was glad that I had already made peace with him and had forgiven him for the things that happened in our marriage.

Washington was very supportive and was there for my children. My ex-in-laws thanked him for stepping in to help raise them. My youngest son struggled for a while, even after his first year of college. Eventually, he got spiritual counseling from the university chaplain. I thank God that he got the help he needed because I didn't know what to do but pray and ask God to help him.

He was on a full-ride scholarship at the University of Louisville, got it together, and took advantage of every *situation. He was team captain of the football team, had pledged Omega Psi Phi Fraternity, and graduated with his bachelor's degree within three years. I was so proud of him! My oldest son dealt with it a little bit differently - he's quiet and reserved. He graduated in May 2019 with his bachelor's degree and wants to be a principal one day. My daughter cried until, eventually, God healed her heart to where she could move on as well. Shortly after his passing, she and my son-in-law welcomed my new granddaughter.*

At this point, 2015, we're enjoying traveling and supporting Jonathan at his high school football games. Then, during the 2018 season of his college season he started preparing to enter the NFL Draft, and his world came to a screeching halt after the first play of the game. He fell back on his wrist and tore three ligaments. After a successful surgery, though, he was out for the season, and I was there, no questions asked. It seemed like so much was being pulled out of me because everybody needed me. I was like all things to all people. But, for my family, I did what was necessary as the matriarch of my home.

Anyway, my son had a plan for his career despite the injury. After he graduated from the University of Louisville, he transferred to the University of Florida, which allowed him to play at a higher level in the SEC. It was a business move to show that he could excel competitively, and he did just that and balled out in the 2019 season. My husband and I were meeting with agents, preparing to put a team together such as a Financial Advisor, CPA, and an Attorney to look over documents to make sure they were legit and that we understood everything.

THINKING OUT LOUD: Even though my relationship with my biological mother failed, I still felt like I needed to meet my biological father. I had hopes of, at least, gaining a relationship with him. After some time, my mother had given me his information and I called him. When he answered, I told him who I was. He sounded a little guarded as if he was thinking, what do you want? During our talks, I let him know that I wasn't there to cause any problems; I just wanted to know him, where I come from, my lineage, etc. The conversations started slow and cold, but he eventually warmed up and started to tell me a little bit more about him. We kept talking, and, eventually, the conversation got better. These conversations went on for a couple of months, and we were gradually opening up more as the relationship grew.

Over time, about a year's time, the relationship had developed into where I was able to meet my biological sisters. My father was married and had two daughters. On New Year's Day 2016, I invited them all to my home. He brought his daughters with him, but his wife did not come at that time. She was trying to take this all in, and I understood. I respected that.

When they arrived, it was a little awkward at first. But my sisters were very cordial with their greeting, and we extended the same. They came in with such good spirits, and we introduced ourselves to each other and exchanged information about ourselves and so forth. We had dinner, took pictures, laughed, talked a little bit more, and then they left. I felt very positive about our meeting. And I see who I resemble, and my children look a lot like my father. The genes are strong, so everybody looks like each other.

I was determined to make another try of connecting with my father. So, here I was again, in 2017, reaching out to him in hopes of getting to know him and build a healthy relationship. I understood that my sisters loved their parents, and to have a bombshell named Carmen dropped on them is explosive and probably was just as nerve-racking as it was for me to find and meet him. I wasn't trying to come between them, but now that they all knew the truth about me, I wanted to be his daughter, too.

That's all I wanted! But I was, of the sort, walking on pins and needles, hoping I wouldn't say or do the wrong thing or make an offensive facial expression, etc. To me, it was much more difficult than I think it should have been. Older and wiser, I know it wasn't my fault that everyone was nervous, but the process had me feeling some kind of way – not good.

After the 2019 season. Jonathan went to the Combine Training at EXOS in Pensacola, FL - he was entering the 2020 NFL Draft. Then, here comes draft day! It was one of the most stressful days in our lives! Especially Jonathan because he had worked so hard to achieve this goal. I taught my children to pray, give it to God and allow Him to direct their path. Because of his wrist injury, his draft stock had dropped a little. But he was a third-round pick. I feel that he is where God destined him to be, and he will do well. As I say, a delay is not a deny - he still made it.

Washington and I had been married before and wanted to start fresh and not make the same mistakes we did in our previous relationships. He was a good man, and he let me be who I was. He had his flaws just like anybody else, and I was able to deal with them. I prayed to God to help us keep our marriage strong because we needed to deliverance from many things. We both loved music, and we traveled everywhere together. Washington depended on me to do a lot of things, especially around the house. He wasn't a handyman-type of guy, so he paid someone to do pretty much everything around the house. His father was absent, but his uncle lived next door. As a man, he lacked in a lot of areas, but he was my man. However, this reminded me of a pattern of choosing guys who were very needy for some reason.

Being a natural nurturer spilled over into my marriages, where it seemed like my husbands needed me like a mom and a wife. When I married Washington, I told him that I did not want to be the man and the woman in the relationship. I needed him to step up to the plate to handle things to take a lot of stress and pressure off of me. I figured out quickly he just wasn't that type of guy, and I had to do a lot for myself. During our marriage, life tried us, tested our faith, our beliefs, and sometimes just left us questioning God. My husband did not have any children - well, he had a stepdaughter from his previous marriage that he raised and loved very much. But he wanted children of his blood. So, I attempted IVF - ALL efforts failed!

I wanted this marriage to be until death does us part, and it was! But I didn't imagine it would be happening at a time where we were in a rough patch. We were getting over some hurdles and through storms before Coronavirus, COVID-19, and other troubles struck again in our lives. It was a whirlwind! For the last six years (2014-2020), my husband had health issues that had gotten worse. When we got married, he already had high blood pressure, high cholesterol, and diabetes. We were making lifestyle changes to bring his numbers down, but Washington struggled with those things. For him, food was his comfort when he would gather with his family, and they ate large consumptions of food. That's how they enjoyed each other's company.

I've always tried to be mindful of my diet. I would pick up weight here and there, but then I would pull back with diet and exercise. As time progressed, I noticed that our sex life was declining. It was semi-non-existent to the point I thought he was having an affair. He wasn't as intimate with me the way that I was used to him coming on to me. Or even with me being romantic, he wasn't responding.

Come to find out, at some point, taking the diabetes and high blood pressure medication had taken its toll on his manhood. Not realizing what was happening, we made an appointment to see a neurologist. At the doctor's appointment, we discovered that the nerves were damaged, and Viagra and Cialis did not help. Washington became withdrawn while we waited to see if things would return to normal.

As a wife, of course, I was dealing with it as well, but I took myself out of the equation to reassure him that I was there with him no matter what. I was unlearned in how deeply impotence affects our husband, sons, men in general, and I needed to educate myself on how to be who he needed me to be. It got so bad until my husband said that he did not want to live anymore. It was very heartbreaking to hear my husband make a statement like that, and all I could do was keep reassuring him that we would get through this. During this time, there was an older co-worker/friend whom I confided in. I was trying to get answers, so I felt comfortable talking with her about it. Come to find out she, made matters worse by telling my husband what I shared with her.

This backstabber wrote a letter to my husband and mailed it to his job! Yes! I said HIS JOB! I was out of town with Jonathan, who was having wrist surgery when this happened. A week before I returned home, my husband called me and stated that he needed to speak with me about something. It was about the letter which said I was complaining to her about how my husband could not satisfy me in the bedroom because he was impotent.

I was in LIVID! I couldn't believe this was happening. I learned a valuable lesson about sharing personal information even with a close friend that some things you have to keep to yourself and talk to the Lord. My husband was devastated and cursed me out. He was screaming and crying over the phone. My heart was broken for him; his pain was unfathomable. I thank God that I wasn't returning home for another week. We needed this time to calm down, collect our thoughts, and deal with our feelings.

Once I returned to Atlanta, he picked me up from the airport, and we didn't say a word to each other until we got almost home. I didn't know what to expect, but I was ready to discuss the situation. He showed me the letter, and I knew where it came from because I never shared that personal with anyone else outside of the home. Immediately, I burned the letter. It was continuing to cause nothing but hardship in the house every time you look at it. At one point, he asked for a divorce because he felt embarrassed and humiliated. I was hurt and remorseful because of the pain and humiliation that I caused him. It took about six months to get past this, and it was a hard lesson learned. Figuring out other ways to show affection towards one another was possible, but, first, I had to regain his trust.

There were times when I felt my body going through a transition. All of a sudden, I would shut down from sex. Maybe it was due to premenopausal and hot flashes; I don't know for sure. But I do know I didn't want to have sex during those times. Being a wife, mother, and pretty much in charge of everything in the household, I was still dealing with my issues but still had to be strong for him and myself. I confronted him about seeking marriage counseling or maybe someone else outside of the marriage that could give us some insight into how to get past this.

He agreed, but he specified that it should be a black male because he would be comfortable talking about what was going on. Our first session was virtual due to the pandemic, so we sat in my office and did a video conference. The therapist made some valid points, asked us some questions, and then asked my husband if he was hearing me and not just listening to me. I think my husband had put up a mental block. No matter what I said or how I expressed my feelings to uplift him, he could not hear me. The counselor told us that there were other ways to please each other. But, based on the outcome of our session, this was not even a thought.

The year 2020 took a turn for this entire nation as a vicious virus, Coronavirus, COVID-19, C19, all of that just took over the lives of many people. This virus affects the respiratory system and other major organs. It is highly contagious, and we have to wear a mask everywhere. Tragedy struck my family head-on with this virus! The weekend before Christmas, about two weeks into our counseling session, Washington went with me to a doctor's appointment about my knee issues. I was not feeling well with flu-like symptoms and an off-and-on fever.

On December 22, 2020, I still wasn't feeling well, then Washington started complaining about the same thing. We went through this for a week. On Christmas Day, we were still not feeling our best as we gathered around my family, including my daughter, granddaughter, son-in-law, my oldest son, and one of my husband's friends who came to visit. We struggled the whole day, and eventually, I just went back to bed.

The day after, I still wasn't feeling my best, and my husband was getting sicker. I decided to take a COVID test at the local Walgreens, and the test was positive. Immediately, I called my daughter and told her they needed to take my granddaughter and get her tested since she was with us a week before Christmas. My daughter was also seven months pregnant, and I was so afraid for her. My granddaughter's test was positive asymptomatic, but my daughter and son-in-law were negative - thank God. My oldest son, who lives with us, tested positive asymptomatic as well.

Washington and I struggled and continued to get sicker. The week after Christmas, his oxygen level started to get low. I called the paramedics, and when they arrived, they checked our vitals. Since we were still talking and our vitals were not in a danger zone, they told us to keep an eye out and call back if it got to a lower level. We had flu symptoms, fever, hives, lesions on our skins, no smell, no taste, pain all over our bodies, etc. We were extremely weak! One morning, my husband said he was hungry, so I attempted to go downstairs to get me some juice and make him a cup of oatmeal in the microwave.

I had to come down about 12 steps to get to the kitchen. I sat down on each step and slid down one by one. By the time I got to the refrigerator, I was so weak. After drinking a cup of orange juice, my stomach started churning. I was dizzy - going in and out. Eventually, I reached for the refrigerator handle and fell straight into the refrigerator, hitting my head. After hitting my head, I fell to the floor, hitting my cheekbone to the hardwood. My oldest son, who lives with us, heard me, and came to my rescue.

On New Year's Eve, I had to call the paramedics again to come and get Washington. This time he decided to go ahead to the hospital. We got him situated in the ambulance, and I gave him a plastic bag with his cell phone charger and extension cord so he could reach his phone while in the bed. Because no one was allowed in the hospital, this would be our only way of communicating. Each morning I video called to check on him. He was doing pretty good with the oxygen mask over his face. I didn't talk long because I wanted him to rest and strengthen his lungs. At one point, the nurse had advised me that he was talking too much to his family. So, I had to step in and let them know that it had to stop; he was doing too much.

The charge nurse was going to take his telephone from him. His family was upset, but, as his wife, I had to make sure my husband was doing all he could to survive. After a week in the hospital, he was beginning to get worse, and the nurse called to explain they were admitting him to ICU and putting him on the ventilator. I wasn't a nurse, but I worked in healthcare for 25 years as an administrator. There were times I had to work in areas such as the ER and outpatient surgery. I also had to take a medical terminology course, so I understood some of the terminologies when I was around the doctors and the nurses. I wasn't too concerned about him going on the ventilator because I understood that was something to allow the patient to breathe and allow the patient lungs to rest.

The ventilator was breathing for him, which could strengthen his lungs. Before he went on the ventilator, the nurse called and wanted me to be on video with him as she explained what was happening. He needed to understand, there couldn't be any gray areas, and they needed his consent. My husband and I prayed together while the nurse stayed on the phone. He was nervous and afraid. He felt like he was going through a dark tunnel and told me he was reaching for me to pull him out. I consoled him to the best of my abilities and said that he would be okay and to pull from my strength, that I would help him come out of the dark tunnel.

When I got off the phone, I remembered we had a counseling session. I called the counselor and was glad I did because I needed to keep my sanity. I was hoping and praying that my husband would recover, so improving myself for me, for him, and our marriage was still a priority even though he was deathly sick. While I was on that phone, about 45-minutes later, the nurse called again to tell me that Washington went into cardiac arrest twice and they had to crack his ribs in the process of reviving him. I was frantic! Just downright scared of losing him. The nurse assured me that she would keep me updated. Although he was in a grave condition, he still had a pulse. About an hour later, I got a call from the hospital, stating that they had arranged for me to come and be beside my husband in ICU.

At first, I didn't know how to take it because they weren't allowing anyone into the hospital. I felt that my husband had passed, and they just wanted to get me up there safely. My son dropped me off, and I told him I would call him back to come and get me later. When I got there, the doctor took me into his office. He told me that my husband had a 50/50 chance of survival, and he was very ill. At this point, the only thing I could do was pray!

As a God-fearing wife, no matter what happened to my husband, and no matter how he would have come out from COVID, whether it be paraplegic or in a rehab facility, I was going to do whatever I could to save him and be there for him till death do us part. I was going to make sure they gave him the best care. He would have everything he needed because I loved him that much that the sex did not even matter anymore.

Washington's battle was fierce on that ventilator; his heart was weak; his lungs were only 40% usage left; his kidneys were failing. I sat by his side daily because they allowed me to come and stay as long as I wanted. I would sing to him, pray, oil his feet and hands while talking to him. They stated that he could hear me even though heavily sedated, but he couldn't respond. However, there were times when the sedation wasn't as heavy, and he would nod his head and attempt to squeeze my hand. I also video-called his sister and his mom from time to time. They told me that a familiar voice could help him fight. Even though his family and I were not on the best of terms at this point, it wasn't about them, it was about my husband surviving, and I did whatever I could to make it happen.

He was on the ventilator for two weeks when they attempted to wean him off. After several tries, he could not do it. At this point, they had to do a tracheotomy which was a success! The next few days, they wanted him to rest in the hopes that some of his vitals would become stable before attempting to do anything else. By now, I was all the way exhausted and went home that Friday evening to rest. The next day when I spoke with the nurse, around 7:00 a.m., not much had changed. He had a catheter, and the nurse advised me that he had not urinated all night. I knew immediately in my heart it was going downhill. I told the nurse that I would be there shortly.

Once I arrived, the doctor was trying to explain what was happening like he always did. I told him he didn't have to update me anymore; I understood what was happening and that my husband's organs were shutting down, and that he'd eventually pass away. The doctor acknowledged that I was correct. This realization had my head spinning - I had to get my mind together. It was happening too fast for me. I asked the doctor to give me a moment because I needed to speak to our children and his family.

Afterward, I decided to take him off the machines, ventilator, dialysis, all the machines. I laid on my husband's chest and told him that I knew he was tired of fighting and that it was okay to go. I would be okay, and I will see him later. On February 1, 2021, after unhooking my husband from the machines, his heart stopped 15 minutes later. I wanted to die with him; a part of me left. It felt like this lost part of me would never come back. Honestly, I think that of all the pain I've experienced in my life, this was the worst kind of pain - ever! Unless you've experienced losing a spouse, I really can't explain it because you become one in the eyes of God.

When we married, it was until death parted us, literally. My life has forever changed; I have to bury my husband. The next day I got up and went to the funeral home to make the arrangements. It was something that I knew I could handle on my own. I picked out everything from the obituary to the cemetery. I wasn't dressed raggedy and looking torn down. I went alone and was intentional about honoring my husband. Facts, Carmen was grieving, but she was looking like Washington took good care of her!

This life event was the hardest thing I ever had to do in my life, and I will never forget it. I truly loved my husband, and he loved me. We both had gone through so much and were at a place where we were genuinely happy. We made plans for our future, we had done so much together, and we were ready to enjoy life, but God had another plan for us. Now, I must figure out what to do and how to go on living without my spouse. The first week after my husband passed, I could not get out of bed. I cried every day all day and only got two hours of sleep. I had a lot of support from friends and friends of my husband.

He knew many people, and they sent food, money, books, candles, etc. Different items in remembrance of him. I had lots of love and support, and this was important! But after a while, it got quiet, and I was alone. I started grief counseling because, for a good four months, nothing looked the same anymore. Even when the sun was shining, it was gloomy and gray to me. Also, while I was grieving, I was still battling an issue from a freak accident that happened on my job back on October 17, 2018.

THINKING OUT LOUD: I was moving things around in my office, and there was a desk drawer with a piece of metal sticking out the side. The desk was defective, trash, and taken out properly. I suffered the consequences of this safety hazard, and a piece of metal went into the shin of my right leg and ripped it wide open. I flipped over the desk, twisted my ankle, and hit the floor. Blood was everywhere – just spewing out of my leg. This accident came out of nowhere and caused me a lot of agonies. I have had three surgeries and one rotator cuff repair.

Eventually, my shin had to be reopened and repaired by a plastic surgeon. Here it is, 2021, and after numerous attempts of cortisone shots and gel injections, I have had a total knee replacement; my right knee was bone on bone with a meniscus tear. This accident has put me through numerous rehabs. And, I have a spine issue with the L1 and L2 sitting on the nerve. Not only that, but I am also dealing with depression. Many people don't like to talk about how real depression is, but it is real-real, which I am managing with the help of the Lord.

Anyway, you know, I am convinced that many people wouldn't understand or probably could not have dealt with not being sexually active for five years. But I loved my husband enough to go through this with him, and I was hoping that we would overcome it. God had another plan, and he called my husband home. There was no way that I would leave my husband just because he could not sexually satisfy me; that never entered my mind.

We were only going through a difficult time, a time that we could have had victory over if he had lived. The strangest thing is that we could go out, we would have a great time, and none of that would even matter until we came home and got ready for bed. My husband turned his back to me every night with his arm crossed, kind of in a fetal position, and went to sleep.

That's when it affected me because even though I knew what he was dealing with, it felt like a rejection of me. Towards the end, I felt like he had just given up. He was dealing with his health issues, weight, family issues, the disrespectful treatment of me by his people, and he did not deal with it. He felt with time, it would fix itself, but it never did. I was tired of being disrespected by his mother for no reason. I felt like he just had so much on his shoulder until he was just tired and was ready to go home to be with the Lord.

CHAPTER 3

HERE I AM

Now here I am, devastated, not understanding what just happened. I had to pray like never before and give it to God and leave it. I sought spiritual and professional counseling. YES! I had to seek counseling! There were days I DID NOT want to live! I felt depleted, but my strength, faith, and trust in God have allowed me to move on in my purpose. It took a minute, but I finally accepted that it was his time to go and not mine. I must live and continue to do what God has for me to do, which is helping others in so many ways, reading His word daily, and many more plans that He has for my future. I say to myself; people may see my glory, but they don't know my story. They need to know the story of my trauma and triumph!

A month after his death, I went on a girl's get-a-way to the beach. It was so relaxing and healing for me to walk the beach listening to the ocean. I took another trip a month later - a quiet 6-day get-a-way. One night in my hotel room, it was about 9:00 p.m., I was lying across the bed crying, asking God why he took my husband. When I dozed off to sleep, I felt something touch my lips. It felt like my husband was kissing me. I slowly opened my eyes and looked around the room, and then closed them. I didn't feel like I was asleep, but I was dreaming, and he came to me. I saw his face, and he was smiling, calling my name, telling me to move on and live.

He told me that he was okay and that I would be okay too and that he loved me. I opened my eyes, and he faded away. It felt so strange, but I knew that this was confirmation that I could live on as a lady and a woman. I was so afraid, though. To even think about dating or marrying anyone else ever again was heart-wrenching. But, from that day forth, I began to regain the strength to live. I prayed to God how I wanted to love again; I'm still young and have a lot of life in me. I ask God to bring the right man into my life who will be for me and will not hurt me.

Also, I asked for the discernment to see things that I could carelessly overlook and that if the person is not to be in my life to keep them away or remove them.

In one of my therapy sessions, I learned that you never get over a loved one's death but learn to live with losing them. Well... I'm living!

THINKING OUT LOUD: In every area of my life (school, church, friendships, and work), I've had some kind of issue dealing with people. I even took a hard look at myself and thought about what I could do to make things better for me when dealing with people. I didn't trust anyone because of my past. If someone asked me for something, I thought there was a motive behind it. If someone did something ill-will to me, I took it to heart, even if it was a mistake on their behalf. I was always guarded and kept to myself.

Once, my ex-ex-husband told me that I was like a beaten and mistreated puppy. So, I was afraid to reach out. Yet, I would get up every day to look my best to impress people who didn't know or care a thing about my inner demons.

I still talk with my biological father and two sisters, and I take what I can get. My children and grandchildren have a relationship with them as well. I came to terms with the fact that you can't force anybody to do anything, and I have to respect that. But I'm human, and I have feelings, and I wish they could walk in my shoes just for two days! No matter how young they were when my mom conceived me, I feel like I'm a constant reminder of their past. I feel like they are ashamed of me, to a certain degree. Right now, though, the best thing that ever happened to me is having my children because I can love them, and they can genuinely love me.

My life has been a roller coaster with high highs and very low lows! The spiritual trauma was deep. Often, I wonder how I've still been able to maintain and keep going. Even though I didn't receive love the way I wanted or needed it, I understand that my adopted mother did what she knew based on her childhood. For sure, my loving motherly instincts automatically kicked in after having babies. By now, I should have been crazy, coo-coo, done lost my mind! But God has made me strong enough to endure. It was By His Grace, no doubt!

With my biological mom, I found a place in my heart for forgiveness. I've never hated her; it was the things she was doing that caused me so much pain to have a relationship with her. However, I made my peace with God, and I reached out to her after she called to give her condolences when my husband passed. I wanted her to know that I loved her but would never allow her to make me feel less than her again. Hopefully, with time we can mend our relationship and, at the least, remain cordial and respectful to one another.

Four years after meeting my father and siblings, my father was communicating better with me and we were bonding well, so I thought, and we were in a good place – so I thought. My father had invited me to his home, and I met his wife, and she has come to my home before. I was satisfied with the progress we were making, and it was helping me heal and progress as well.

However, when holidays come around, I am not a part of his family gatherings. I have to see it from a distance - social media. We all have met, so I ask, why am I still not "part of the whole" family? Although I don't know the answer, I do know, understand, and accept that my life - just the way it is - was ordained by God. I know that all these experiences were part of my purpose to help someone else. My relationship started changing with my father, and I noticed that my sisters were not as social about me as I was about them.

For example, we would take photos together at lunch or what have you, and they never posted any pictures of me or tagged me in anything on their social media page. I would put maybe one or two posts up to say I had lunch with my sisters, etc. I understand that people are private and may not want to expose sensitive things, and they have the right to display what they want on social media. But they never mentioned me.

But when your father allows something to happen to make you feel like you are a nobody, that's when I have to draw the line. I noticed that his words and actions were in a major conflict. Recently, I was invited to a family celebration with all of his family and friends etc. We had seating arrangements, and I was seated with my oldest son in the very back corner of the room, away from everybody (my son was my escort to the event).

Once he noticed what they did, he told me we were leaving because I didn't deserve to be mishandled like that. It was difficult dealing with this because I never felt accepted growing up. I always felt like an outcast, just trying to fit in somewhere. It was a 'slap in the face reminder' that I am an outside child, his little secret, and will never be accepted by his family.

It was an insult, and my feelings were hurt, but I got over it. How? I had recalled a time in my early teens when I would pray for God to please let me meet my biological parents. God granted me that wish, but he also showed me why I was in foster care and adopted. I'm more grounded and spiritually rooted. I have a heart of love, acceptance, non-judgmental, and a caring spirit. Nothing else matters if your heart is not right and no love for God. Regardless of what I experienced; God covered me.

God kept me, kept my mind, and I can appreciate all that I've experienced. This situation taught me that you never have to be tolerated by anybody and never let anybody make you feel like you're nothing when you are somebody. I pray for both of my biological parents that God touches their hearts because they can't love me wholeheartedly and treat me like I'm an embarrassment to them.

At this point in my life, I am determined to put closure to this chapter of wanting to have a healthy relationship with my biological parents. I hold no animosity towards them but wish things were better than they are. It just would have been nice if they had considered my feelings on every level. It was a depressing situation, and for me, I had to pray harder each day as I felt as if I got the short end of the deal; plus, I didn't want this generational curse to affect my family. God knew how much I could bear. In therapy, I was taught that we should not have any expectations of people - it lessens the level of disappointments. It's the truth! So, now, I don't expect anything.

Anyways, I am finally peeling off the layers of pain and disappointment and have surrendered this desire to God because it was too much for me to handle. I am grown, now, I have matured, and I turned out just fine. My father is God!

I often wonder if adults understand that the negative things that they do to children break them in many ways. So many times, parents teach us to be respectful and to do the right thing. Yet, many of us, including me, have suffered from something that an adult did to us. For me, it wasn't always the physical harm, but my mind was a battlefield. I try to block out some of the things that happened to me, but some of those same things tend to cross my mind and oppress me. I understand it can be a lot as a parent dealing with issues as an adult, based on what happened to them as a child. You would think they would try to get it right with their child. Some do, others don't, and some deal with it to a certain degree.

To the young people growing up in foster care or adults who have dealt with rejection from parents and family, YOU ARE NOT ALONE! God is with you at all times. I have to tell myself this from time to time when I feel lonely for family, other than my children. I see many adults, who were adopted, have a lot of issues with acceptance, trust, anger, and so forth. I've met several adoptees, and we have a lot in common. I want to remind you that family can be your best friend, a stranger you meet in the grocery store, or a person you break bread with. Again, YOU ARE NOT ALONE!

The worse thing that happened to me was losing my husband and the way he passed from COVID. Even though my friends and children support me, I still get sad and depressed because I miss my husband. I love him, still. Although I don't know what the future holds, I'm sure like hell getting myself together again. I pray that this testimony has inspired and uplifted you. I want to encourage mothers and fathers (who have experienced a childhood like mine, in foster care or not) to not give up.

You are here for a purpose and on purpose! Figure out what your purpose in life is and go for it. I believe that our latter days will be greater and better because there is so much that we can positively pour into others. For certain, though, this journey to greater and better has made me question God many times. Yet, By His Grace... Here I am!

~ THE FRUIT OF MY WOMB ~

The hardships I experienced in my entire life were extremely difficult. But today, I see the bigger picture. I tell you the truth, though, you must be careful what you ask God for because when He gives it to you, you have to be ready to receive and endure. Well, let me tell you something - I WAS NOT Ready! But, ready-or-not, I still wanted to meet my biological parents, and I did. I believed that my life would have been better if they raised me. However, I understand that it had to be what it was.

Although my family dynamics were not the ideal family environment, I learned a lot of valuable lessons growing up. I think the most important one was how to be a lady and how to be a good mother. I learned how to cook and clean, and I discovered God and His love for me by my mother taking me to church every Sunday, Wednesday night bible study, and allowing me to sing in the choir. Those things shaped and molded me to be the Carmen that I am today. I do not believe that I would have had those same opportunities if my biological parents reared me.

Nothing could have prepared me for losing my husband. That bulging pain was like a twisting knife stuck in my heart - the worst pain ever! But just as God healed and delivered me from so many other traumas, I am healing, am healed, from this pain. My husband will forever be in my heart, and I miss him dearly. With the spiritual and professional counseling I've received, I am confident in living in my healing. I am confident in moving forward with my life. I thank God for my three beautiful children who stand with and support me, keeping me strong. I've learned some valuables on this journey. I've learned that it doesn't matter what people think of me because they're going to form their own opinion regardless. It only matters what God thinks of me because I'm only here to please God and not man. I've learned to forgive, even though I might not forget. Past experiences can teach you to be a better person and not treat others negatively.

My motto in life is to do unto others as you would have them do unto you. I've learned to show a heart of love and compassion and to think before I speak. I go to God in prayer when I'm bothered. He is the only one that can fix whatever it is that is bothering me. I've learned to appreciate life and live one day at a time because tomorrow is not a promise, a guarantee.

I've learned that it's okay to help others, but there are limits to everything. I thank God for His grace and mercy because the outcome of my life could have been abortion, and none of us would be here to read this testimony. But my biological mother decided to give me the gift of life, and I'm thankful for that.

Another thing I learned on this journey called life is that if you don't have anyone else (whether you know you don't or you believe you don't), be aware that God is there! He still sits high and looks low, and there is no doubt in my mind that He has been with me through it all.

Carmen Y. Greenard-Varnum

IN MEMORY OF
WASHINGTON VARNUM
IN MY HEART FOREVER

To learn more about the woman, the wife, the mother, and the author, visit her via social media and email at

Facebook: Carmen Greenard Varnum
Twitter: @varnum_carmen
carmenvarnum@yahoo.com

Made in the USA
Columbia, SC
25 February 2025